LIFEWITHOUTLIMBS

—— 31 DAYS TO A ——

HOPE INSPIRED

—— LIFE ——

BY NICK VUJICIC · LIFE WITHOUT LIMBS

31 Days to a Hope Inspired Life
Published by Life Without Limbs
P.O. Box 2430
Agoura Hills, CA 91376

Italics in Scripture quotations reflect the author's added emphasis.

Details in some anecdotes and stories have been changed to protect the
identities of the persons involved.

ISBN 978-0-9889876-0-9

Copyright © 2013 by Nick Vujicic

Cover design by PlainJoe Studios; cover photography by Ed McGowan.
Content editing and project supervision provided by Roger Kemp and
Company, Inc.

Published in the United States by Life Without Limbs, Agoura Hills, California.

LIFEWITHOUTLIMBS

31 DAYS TO A

HOPE INSPIRED

LIFE

BY NICK VUJICIC · LIFE WITHOUT LIMBS

INTRODUCTION

31 DAYS TO A HOPE INSPIRED LIFE

I hear it all the time. *"I hope it doesn't rain."* Or, *"I hope we win."*

But is the essence of hope really limited to statements like, *"I hope it doesn't rain?"* Sounds a lot more like a *wish* than *hope* to me!

When you look up the word hope in the dictionary, the first definition you'll find reads, *"The feeling that events will turn out for the best."* I imagine this is probably the first thing most people think of when we hear the word *hope*. But I'm going to tell you right up front—it's not the kind of hope I'm interested in! No, we have more than enough *wishful thinking* going around these days.

But look through the other definitions in the dictionary and you'll find a richer meaning for this word. Hope can be described as *"a person or thing in which expectations are centered."* Now, that's what I'm talking about! It's the kind of hope that's centered in the person of Jesus Christ.

What are you hoping for today? Good weather? A positive outcome? Hey, let's take it a little deeper.

Maybe there's a relationship that needs to be healed. Or you're longing for a deeper sense of significance and belonging. Whatever you're hoping for, fix your expectations in the only One who deserves our trust. If you're placing your hope in anyone or anything other than Jesus, that's not hope at all. It's *wishful thinking*!

Psalm 31:24 says, *"Be strong and let your heart take courage, All you who hope in the LORD"* (NASB). And here's another verse I love: *"May the God of hope fill you with all joy and peace in believing, so that by the power of the Holy Spirit you may abound in hope"* (Romans 15:13 NIV).

Over the next thirty-one days we're going on a journey to find hope. Not a temporary hope that lasts so long as we're feeling optimistic. An unwavering, unretracting, expectation-filled hope in Jesus Christ!

DAY ONE
FIRST DAY OF SCHOOL

Go figure. As a little kid, I didn't really realize I was different until I showed up to my first day of school.

That first day of kindergarten was a disaster! My mom remembers how I couldn't stop crying. See, I was born without arms and legs. And growing up, my parents treated me just like a normal kid. Because I *was* a normal kid! Apparently my classmates couldn't handle the shock of seeing a kid without limbs. Some laughed. Some freaked out. Others just avoided me.

This experience was just the beginning of a long journey toward finding my identity. I've had my ups and downs, and even a season of depression in my teen years. But through it all, I've learned to let *God* define me. Not others who see me.

Now that I'm an adult, I've grown familiar with double takes. Everywhere I go, I can feel people glancing in my direction. But here's what God has done. He's taught me to use those otherwise awkward moments for His glory. He's taught me to catch people's eyes and to smile back until they smile, too.

Life without limbs has opened up incredible opportunities to touch people, and meet them in their weakness. Jesus taught me to smile, to talk and to reflect His love. And by the way, once I got to know my little kindergarten buddies, we got along just fine!

"You will be secure, because there is hope; you will look about you and take your rest in safety."

Job 11:18 NIV

DAY TWO

HOW COME YOU SMILE SO MUCH?

People often ask me, *"Nick, how come you smile so much?"*

Well, it hasn't always been this way. These days, I've got lots to smile about. In fact, my friends tell me I'm *irrepressible*. But when I was young, not so much. Most kids feel a little insecure, but I really struggled with my fears. Other kids kept telling me I wasn't good enough, reinforcing my own doubts that I would never amount to anything. And I got down, man. Seriously depressed.

No one was more shocked than my parents when they gave birth to a little boy without arms and legs. No one saw it coming. Three ultrasounds and all the doctors missed it. Life without limbs is tough to deal with.

As a kid, I eventually learned to cope with the teasing. But there came a time in my own heart when I really wondered if I could go on. At my lowest moment, God taught me to smile. It was nothing I did for myself. It's what Jesus did for me.

So now when people ask, *"Hey, Nick, how come you smile so much?"* I'm ready with an answer. I smile because I'm loved. And second, I smile because everything's going to be okay.

Hey, when the world says you're not good enough, get a second opinion. Ask Jesus. He'll give you every reason in the world to smile.

"Surely you have granted him eternal blessings and made him glad with the joy of your presence."

Psalm 21:6 NIV

DAY THREE

THE "I" WORD

Ever had someone crush your dream? It sounds something like this: *"What? You wanna do what? You gotta be kiddin' me! You're outta your mind!"* Then they drop the I-bomb. They say, *"That's **impossible!**"* It's especially painful when someone we respect lets this ominous word slip out.

Well, I'm just stubborn enough, just old enough, just seasoned enough to quit paying attention to the word *impossible*. God's given me a filter for dismissing the I-word! Because I know that with God *nothing is impossible!*

Imagine how my mom and dad felt. When I was born, they were overwhelmed, big time. You can't blame them! They couldn't imagine having the strength and patience to take care of a limbless little boy. But God stepped in and graciously provided everything they needed.

What's got you down today? What's overwhelming you? What stands in your way today as an impossibility? Have you ever noticed the first two letters in the word *impossible*? Yeah, I-M. Me, me, me.

It's time to take your eyes off yourself and fix them on the only One who can conquer any challenge.

When you do this, you'll discover the greatest power in all of life. With God all things are possible. He can do it! That's the reason we can say with full confidence, *"I can do all things through Him who strengthens me"* (Philippians 4:13 NASB).

"I can do all things through Him who strengthens me."

Philippians 4:13 NASB

DAY FOUR

WINNING AT LIFE

I just love sports! I love the competition and that exciting energy you feel when a team works together for victory.

If you play soccer, football or any other competitive sport, you know the thrill of winning. There's nothing better than defeating your opponent and clinching a title! In fact, sometimes I feel like God *designed* us to win!

When it comes to spiritual matters, God wants every one of us to be conquerors. And He's provided a way for that to happen! But victory in life doesn't necessarily come to those who are talented or athletic. It doesn't come from being the most intelligent or the wealthiest. It doesn't even come to those who play the game right.

No, victory comes when you surrender it all to Jesus Christ.

Have you made that decision yet? No matter what you've done, no matter what kind of dirt you may have in your past, the victory is yours when you say, "*Jesus, forgive me of my sins. I need you. Come into my life and change me."*

Are you ready to let Him in? Are you ready to give up trying to win at life on your own? Romans 8:37 says, *"We are more than conquerors through him who loved us"* (NIV).

It's time for you to give up the fight. Turn your battles over to the only One who can fight on your behalf. And when you finally do, He will make sure you win. Big time.

"We are more than conquerors through him who loved us."

Romans 8:37 NIV

DAY FIVE

HIGH HOPES FOR HEAVEN

Imagine a place where every curse is reversed—no more sickness, no more pain. Everything is beautiful and the joy never ends. That's where I'd like to be!

When's the last time you thought about heaven? I don't mean just a passing thought, but really sat down to think about what life is gonna be like in eternity? I have to tell you, I think about it all the time! Don't get me wrong. I love my life and all the opportunities I have to make a difference on earth. But even the greatest joys are nothing compared to what we'll experience when we meet Jesus face-to-face and live with Him forever.

In Revelation 21:4 we read that in heaven God *"will wipe every tear from [our] eyes. There will be no more death or mourning or crying or pain"* (NIV).

All the fears, the pain, difficulty, sorrow and wounds we experience right now will all become a distant memory when we join our Savior in heaven. And just think, all our physical ailments will be healed! I look forward to the day when I have arms and legs to run and jump and dance for joy over what my God has done.

So how about you? Do you look forward to heaven? If you believe in Jesus Christ, you have an amazing future ahead of you! Let that truth transform your life right now and give you hope.

Oh yeah, there's one more thing I look forward to when I get to heaven. And that's getting the opportunity to see you there! It's gonna be great!

"He will wipe every tear from their eyes. There will be no more death or mourning or crying or pain, for the old order of things has passed away."

Revelation 21:4 NIV

DAY SIX

GOD IS ENOUGH

A wise friend once said to me, *"Nicky, you may not have hands to hold your wife's hand, but you don't need hands to hold her heart!"* These wise words were a powerful reminder to me that God is sufficient. He meets our every need.

I've asked God for a lot of different things in my life. I don't know if you've ever asked Him, *"God, can I please have a million dollars?"* Well, my prayer was this: *"God, will you please give me arms and legs?"* I've come to realize that our version of what we need rarely reflects God's perfect plan. Our vision is so cloudy, so limited.

On the outside, I'm a little different than most people. But on the inside, I'm *painfully normal*. I struggle just like you do. But I've come to trust that God knows what's best for me, and He provides everything I really need! This attitude kind of takes people off guard. At first they can't figure me out. They don't understand my smile or the sparkle in my eyes. Hey, it's nothing I've done. It's what Christ has done *in* me.

No matter what circumstances come your way, God's grace is enough. And He has a purpose for your life. Jesus said,

"My grace is sufficient for you, for my power is made perfect in weakness" (2 Corinthians 12:9 NIV).

Whatever your plight, God is enough. He will meet your every need.

"My grace is sufficient for you, for my power is made perfect in weakness."

2 Corinthians 12:9 NIV

DAY SEVEN

TEARS IN A BOTTLE

When was the last time you had a good cry? I mean, a real good eyelid-flippin' cry?

A lot of guys my age think tears are a sign of weakness. When you show that kind of emotion, it's considered wimpy and unmanly. The last thing you want is to be caught boo-hooing in front of your friends.

But I'll confess I've spent a fair amount of private moments in tears. Sometimes it's sadness. Sometimes it's fear. Sometimes it's disappointment or even anger. But the best kind of tears come when you just stop and admit to God that you're done. The best tears flow when you realize you're completely inadequate.

I'm not talking about having some kind of spoiled brat outburst. I'm talking about those sacred moments between you and God when you tell him He is God and you are not. When you admit that you cannot do this thing on your own. I can tell you from experience, when you reach that valley of brokenness, that's when the growing and the healing begins.

Psalm 56:8 says, "*[God], you have put my tears in Your bottle*" (NASB).

Are you emotionally depleted today? At the end of yourself? Feeling finished? God knows. He hasn't missed one single teardrop. And Revelation 21:4 says a day is coming when "*He will wipe away every tear from their eyes; and there will no longer be any death; there will no longer be any mourning, or crying, or pain.*"

Friend, He's storing your tears in a bottle. And He's ready to let the healing begin.

"[God], you have put my tears in Your bottle."

Psalm 56:8 NASB

DAY EIGHT
OUR PAIN IS NOT WASTED

While preaching at a church in Orange County, California, I was telling the congregation that God can use our circumstances to encourage others. And that's when I noticed a little boy in the crowd. I asked the father to bring his son up on the platform and we held him up. He was just a baby. Tears swept across the room and there wasn't a dry eye in the place.

I couldn't believe it. Like me, my new friend was born without arms and without legs, with a little chicken drumstick like mine. He had a couple of toes on one side and that's it. This little boy was the firstborn son of two loving and frightened parents. They had no medical explanation and like my parents, no warning.

God orchestrated a beautiful day for us. My mum and dad were with me from Australia and they met the boy's parents. You can imagine their exchange! My folks had an opportunity to bring hope and light to a young mother and father who felt all alone.

They told me that this little boy watches my DVD sometimes three times a day, and he says, *"Nick! Nick!*

Nick!" We spent a whole day together skateboarding, playing with toys and rolling around on the carpet.

I've always told God, *"If you made me without arms and legs so I could reach just one more soul, then it's worth it all."* And now, in the eyes of this little unsuspecting boy, I've seen God's answer.

"Blessed be the God and Father of our Lord Jesus Christ, the Father of mercies and God of all comfort, who comforts us in all our affliction so that we will be able to comfort those who are in any affliction with the comfort with which we ourselves are comforted by God."

---

2 Corinthians 1:3-4 NASB

DAY NINE
GOD'S PERFECT CREATION

One of my most popular videos on *YouTube* shows footage of me skateboarding, surfing, hitting a golf ball, falling down, getting up and best of all, receiving hugs from all sorts of great people.

Why do you think those *YouTube* clips have been viewed millions of times? Well, the comment I hear most often goes something like this: *"When a guy without arms and legs can be so happy, it makes me wonder why I feel sorry for myself."* Implied in those comments is the idea that *"if Nick can do it and smile, I should be able to do it, too."*

So why do I smile? I smile because I believe I'm God's perfect creation, designed precisely according to His plan. And so are you. In Psalm 139:14 we read, *"I praise you because I am fearfully and wonderfully made"* (NIV).

You are God's beautiful creation. He made you for a purpose. Your life cannot be limited any more than God's love can be contained. Hey, I'm officially *disabled* but I'm truly *enabled* because of my lack of limbs. If that's true for me, imagine what God has planned for you!

"I praise you because I am fearfully and wonderfully made."

Psalm 139:14 NIV

DAY TEN
BURDENS INTO BLESSINGS

Life can be unfair. Sometimes it's just plain old painful. But no matter what we've been through, we don't have to live like a victim.

Hard times and tough circumstances can trigger self-doubt and despair in our hearts. I understand that all too well. But the Bible says, *"Consider it pure joy, my brothers, whenever you face trials of many kinds"* (James 1:2 NIV). I struggled many years to learn that hard lesson.

It all started coming together when I began to see my disability, my burden, as a blessing. Believe me, it didn't happen overnight! Some of those dark passages in the early years were daunting. But eventually, I emerged from despair and embraced hope instead. It's a far better way to live.

What are you facing today? What has set you back and caused you to act like a victim? Has someone betrayed you? Have you begun to second-guess your value? Do you feel like God has completely overlooked you?

When you trust in our Heavenly Father, know this—the victory doesn't come when your circumstances change. The victory doesn't arrive when you muster up the strength. The victory comes when you realize with all of your being that you can't do this on your own.

It's time for you to surrender. Ask God to help you see your burden as a blessing. Isaiah 40:31 says, *"Those who hope in the LORD will renew their strength. They will soar on wings like eagles; they will run and not grow weary, they will walk and not be faint."*

"Those who hope in the LORD will renew their strength. They will soar on wings like eagles; they will run and not grow weary, they will walk and not be faint."

Isaiah 40:31 NIV

DAY ELEVEN
MORE PRECIOUS THAN DIAMONDS

I can't hide it. Just by looking at me, people know that I've faced a few hardships along the way. But my *burden*, or what some see as a disability, has become a *blessing* in disguise.

It's been incredible to see how God's perfect design for my disabled body has opened countless doors of opportunity. People in all walks of life are eager to hear what I have to say. And it gives me occasion to communicate the power of God's love and hope in Jesus Christ to unsuspecting people.

What's holding you back right now? Do you feel forgotten? Like an outcast? Sidelined because of some stupid mistakes you've made? I can't put a hand on your shoulder to reassure you, but I can speak from my heart. As God's child, you are beautiful and precious, worth more than all the diamonds in the world.

That's not idle psychobabble. That's true! I love this paraphrase of Romans 8:29: *"God knew what he was doing from the very beginning. He decided from the outset to shape the lives of those who love him along the same lines as the life of his Son"* (THE MESSAGE).

We serve the King of Creation who doesn't make mistakes. Whatever burdens you're carrying right now, give them to God. You'll be amazed how God can use your precious life for His glory.

"God knew what he was doing from the very beginning. He decided from the outset to shape the lives of those who love him along the same lines as the life of his Son."

Romans 8:29 THE MESSAGE

DAY TWELVE
WIDOWS AND ORPHANS

Every little boy on the planet needs a daddy. Every little girl deserves a mommy. But we live in a broken world and tragically, lots of little kids cry themselves to sleep at night, all alone.

I'm not talking about third world countries. Yes, I've been to many of those places, and lots of kids have lost touch with their parents. But you don't have to look very far in our own country to find boys and girls estranged from one or both parents! Just look up and down your street or maybe at school. There's someone, somewhere, *who needs you.*

The Bible clearly reminds us that when we see a need, it's our role to step in! Listen to this warning in James 1:26-27: *"Anyone who sets himself up as 'religious' by talking a good game is self-deceived. This kind of religion is hot air and only hot air. Real religion, the kind that passes muster before God the Father, is this: Reach out to the homeless and loveless in their plight"* (THE MESSAGE).

Okay, it's time to get real. This verse doesn't sound like an option, but a command! So let's ask God to help us identify someone who needs us—maybe a fatherless child or a widow who's lonely—and do something. It's time to quit bluffing and get real with our faith. Real religion is this: *"To visit orphans and widows in their affliction"* (ESV). Look for people who need love, and let them know it's going to be okay. Because with Jesus, there's hope.

"Anyone who sets himself up as 'religious' by talking a good game is self-deceived. This kind of religion is hot air and only hot air. Real religion, the kind that passes muster before God the Father, is this: Reach out to the homeless and loveless in their plight."

James 1:26-27 THE MESSAGE

DAY THIRTEEN
MY LEFT FOOT

One of my personal heroes is an overcomer—the late Christy Brown. Born in Dublin, Ireland in 1932, Christy was the tenth of thirteen children. Unlike me, he entered the world with all of his limbs. But he was terribly crippled—so much so that he couldn't move and could barely utter a sound. Later in life, he was formally diagnosed with a severe form of cerebral palsy.

Because he couldn't speak, doctors concluded that Christy was also mentally handicapped. But his mother insisted he was quite bright and capable. He began to emerge with special talents like swimming and then writing, drawing and painting. He used the only appendage on his body that worked—his left foot.

As a young adult, Christy was fascinated by literature. Several famous Irish writers inspired him to express himself as a poet and author. His first book was a memoir called My Left Foot. Recognize the title? It was later expanded into a novel and made into a feature film. Daniel Day-Lewis won an Oscar for his portrayal of Christy Brown.

If Christy could accomplish these feats by moving only one part of his tormented body, imagine what God has in store for you!

Your story has yet to be written. You are not a victim of your limitations.

"'For I know the plans I have for you,' declares the LORD, 'plans to prosper you and not to harm you, plans to give you hope and a future'" (Jeremiah 29:11 NIV).

"'For I know the plans I have for you,' declares the LORD, 'plans to prosper you and not to harm you, plans to give you hope and a future.'"

Jeremiah 29:11 NIV

DAY FOURTEEN
EARTHQUAKE RESCUE

Do you have days when you feel trapped? Nowhere to turn? Like you're losing hope?

The dust has settled on the devastating 2009 earthquake in Haiti. In the aftermath, countless stories of courage and hope have surfaced. Marie's powerful story is just one inspiring example of these accounts.

Her son, Emmanuel, was believed to be among the dead buried beneath the rubble. The twenty-one-year-old tailor had been with his mother in her apartment building when the earthquake hit. Marie managed to escape, but no one could find Emmanuel.

Several days passed. Hope was beginning to dwindle while emergency crews worked non-stop to remove layers and layers of concrete. At one point, Marie was certain she heard her son's voice faintly calling out for help.

She convinced an experienced team of international engineers to cut through the concrete, steel and debris at the exact spot where she heard the voice. Ten days after the earthquake, they spotted Emmanuel's hand, then his body. Though severely dehydrated, hungry and traumatized, he survived.

Are you losing hope? Let me assure you, God hears your cry. Even in your private lonely moments, He hears you! He knows your name. And He's ready to rescue you.

Don't lose heart. As Paul said to the Romans, *"May the God of hope fill you with all joy and peace as you trust in him, so that you may overflow with hope by the power of the Holy Spirit"* (Romans 15:13 NIV).

"May the God of hope fill you with all joy and peace as you trust in him, so that you may overflow with hope by the power of the Holy Spirit."

Romans 15:13 NIV

"Yet this I call to mind and therefore I have hope: Because of the LORD's great love we are not consumed, for his compassions never fail. They are new every morning; great is your faithfulness."

Lamentations 3:21-23 NIV

Be strong and let your heart take courage, All you who hope in the LORD.

Psalm 31:24 NASB

"Through him we have also obtained access by faith into this grace in which we stand, and we rejoice in hope of the glory of God."

Romans 5:2 ESV

DAY FIFTEEN
SURF'S UP

We sat on the beach in Hawaii, two limbless friends swapping stories.

A few years ago, I had the privilege of meeting the world-class surfer, Bethany Hamilton. You may recall her gripping story. She was attacked by a tiger shark, resulting in the loss of her left arm.

Bethany was just thirteen when the near-death incident occurred. That morning, she lost seventy percent of her blood. Bethany told me how she just kept praying as they rushed her to a hospital forty-five minutes away. Her paramedic kept whispering into her ear, *"God will never leave you or forsake you."*

When they finally arrived at the hospital, Bethany was fading fast. You'll never guess who was at the hospital getting ready for knee surgery. Her own father! They immediately switched the patients, father for daughter, and the procedure saved her life. Amazingly, Bethany bounced back faster than anyone expected. She was out surfing again just three weeks after the attack.

Instead of feeling sorry for herself, Bethany surrendered her life to God's will. She believes with all her heart that the loss she experienced was part of God's master plan for her life.

Are you feeling desperate today? Like your spirit is hemorrhaging and you're running out of options? I love this paraphrase of Deuteronomy 31:6. *"Be strong. Take courage. Don't be intimidated. Don't give them a second thought because God, your God, is striding ahead of you. He's right there with you. He won't let you down; he won't leave you"* (THE MESSAGE).

"Be strong. Take courage. Don't be intimidated. Don't give them a second thought because God, your God, is striding ahead of you. He's right there with you. He won't let you down; he won't leave you."

Deuteronomy 31:6 THE MESSAGE

DAY SIXTEEN
WHO VALIDATES YOU?

Where do you find your validation? Who gives you a sense of belonging, purpose and meaning?

I can't imagine that any previous generation has been lied to as much as ours. We're continually bombarded with seductive messages. We're told that we need to have a certain look, buy a certain car, and attain a certain lifestyle in order to be successful. Hey, it's all a bunch of baloney!

Too many people settle for superficial meaning when they buy into the extremes of narcissism and self-indulgence. Going down the road of instant gratification is a one-way street that leads to a dead end. No wonder more celebrities are in rehab than in church! Too many of them worship the false gods of vanity, pride and lust.

As a kid, my parents instilled in me a confidence that Jesus loves me. They taught me that my disability was all part of God's master plan for my life. And I would be humming along fine until some snotty nosed kid ran up to me and screamed, *"Nick, you're a freak!"*

Life can be cruel. People can be thoughtless or just plain mean. So I learned to seek my validation from the only One qualified to give it. Friend, you are a child of God!

The apostle Paul said, *"God's Spirit touches our spirits and confirms who we really are. We know who He is, and we know who we are: Father and children"* (Romans 8:16 THE MESSAGE*).*

"God's Spirit touches our spirits and confirms who we really are. We know who He is, and we know who we are: Father and children."

Romans 8:16 THE MESSAGE

DAY SEVENTEEN
DID I DO SOMETHING WRONG?

If you're suffering today, physically, emotionally, or financially, it's possible you find yourself wondering if God is punishing you.

I was fifteen when I first heard the story about the blind man in John chapter 9. He had been blind since birth. And when Jesus' disciples saw him, they asked, *"Who sinned? This man? Or his parents?"*

It was the same question I had asked myself. *"How come I was born without arms and legs? Did I do something wrong? Did my parents do something wrong?"*

Listen to Jesus' response. This is *ridiculously* good! He said, *"Neither this man nor his parents sinned … but this happened so the works of God might be displayed in his life"* (John 9:3 NIV).

Did you hear that? Jesus took the parents right off the hook. No guilt. But even better, He assured this man that God allowed his blindness so *"the works of God might be displayed in him"*! How cool is *that*?

When I heard that story, it was a game-changer for me. I began to discover God's amazing and intentional plan for my life. I saw new possibilities. I realized that I was not being punished. No, I was custom-made so that God could be seen in me!

And you were, too. Whatever you're going through today, God never makes mistakes. You are custom-made according to His plan! He wants nothing more than to reflect His glory through *you*.

"'Neither this man nor his parents sinned,' said Jesus, 'but this happened so the works of God might be displayed in his life.'"

John 9:3 NIV

DAY EIGHTEEN

WE ARE GOD'S MASTERPIECE

I don't know where you live, but where I'm from, it's the land of beautiful people.

Yeah, I live in Southern California. Movie stars. Paparazzi. In the Golden State, people spend lots of time, money and energy perfecting their look. Bronze tans, buff bodies, expensive cars—you get the picture. I have to admit, sometimes I find all the pretty people downright intimidating.

Most of us struggle with our physical confidence to some extent. Perhaps you wrestle with an inner dialogue that condemns you saying, *I'm too fat. I'm too short. My nose is too big.* But you know what? The gorgeous people are struggling, too. They're often putting on a public charade, hiding their private fears.

Hey, when we're unwilling to accept ourselves as God sees us, we're less willing to accept others. It all breaks down when we believe the lie. And the lie leads to loneliness and isolation.

Listen to this verse in Ephesians 2—proof that God crafted you according to His plan! It says, *"For we are*

God's masterpiece. He has created us anew in Christ Jesus, so we can do the good things he planned for us long ago" (Ephesians 2:10 NLT).

Take heart, my friend. No matter your age, whether you live in Southern California or northern Maine, you are God's masterpiece, created for *His* glory.

"For we are God's masterpiece. He has created us anew in Christ Jesus, so we can do the good things he planned for us long ago."

Ephesians 2:10 NLT

DAY NINETEEN

WE ARE GOD'S AMBASSADORS

Don't you think this world would be a better place if the paparazzi quit wasting their time chasing down movie stars sneaking out of rehab centers? Call it wishful thinking, but what if their cameras were focused instead on college grads with advanced degrees, or relief workers bringing medicine to the poor? Nah … not likely. The media loves to catch the rich and famous fall from grace.

But not everyone is obsessed with plastic surgery, liposuction and Rolex watches. As I travel around the country, I get to meet all kinds of people who've given their lives to serving others, loving their neighbor, and giving praise to God.

Looking outward rather than inward, living outside our skin, is God's design for healthy living. Have you begun to master the art of selflessness? Hey, it's not a natural expression. Only God can help us get beyond ourselves! And it happens right when we place our faith and trust in Jesus Christ.

In 2 Corinthians 5:17 and 20, Paul said, *"Therefore, if anyone is in Christ, he is a new creation; the old has gone, the new has come! We are therefore Christ's ambassadors!"* (NIV). Did you catch that? We are God's *ambassadors*. That means we are His royal messengers! What an awesome privilege!

Hey, let's give the paparazzi something much better to look at. Let's live like people who've been transformed from the inside out—God's people doing God's work in God's name!

"Therefore, if anyone is in Christ, he is a new creation; the old has gone, the new has come! We are therefore Christ's ambassadors!"

---

2 Corinthians 5:17, 20 NIV

DAY TWENTY

THE ART OF ASKING A GOOD QUESTION

Few skills will transform your relationships any more than asking a good question. It's a cultivated art form, and a rare virtue in our culture. Most people want to be heard but rarely do they stop to listen. We live in a generation of teens, children, even husbands and wives who desperately need a listening friend.

The first four books in the New Testament describe the dynamic life of Jesus. When you read through these accounts, it's amazing how many times Jesus spoke to His friends with questions. In his encounters with different people, Jesus always posed a question that was like a laser beam to the heart. He intuitively saw through the veneer of someone's skin and looked right into their soul. He would cut to the chase and say, *"Do you want to get well?"* (John 5:6 NIV). *"Why are you so afraid?"* (Matthew 8:26). Or, to the boy, *"How many loaves do you have?"* (Matthew 15:34). He would ask a direct question, let His words hang in the air, and He would listen.

What was the outcome? People felt understood. They spoke to Jesus and received what they desperately needed. We need to learn the art of asking good questions the way Jesus did. Then, wait for the answer. You'll be amazed by what you learn.

"He who answers before listening – that is his folly and shame."

Proverbs 18:13 NIV

DAY TWENTY-ONE
HEAVEN IS OUR FOREVER-HOME

Steve Jobs, the iconic leader at Apple, was a man who never gave up on his dream.

When you read Steve's biography, you learn how many times he stepped up to plate, swung for the fence and *struck out.* Sometimes his failed ventures cost him millions of dollars. But he dusted himself off and kept trying. And Apple ignited a revolution in the tech business. His successes impacted the world!

I won't speak to Steve's spiritual walk, because that's between him and God. But I can say that when he died of cancer, it occurred to me that even the richest, most successful men in the world can't beat the odds. *Ten out of every ten people die.* Staggering stats!

Early in his life, Steve told his employees to work like they were going to die tomorrow. Let me suggest a better alterative. Let's live like we're going to live *forever.* That's the promise God gives to those who know His Son, Jesus Christ. Yeah, we're going to pass from this life to the next. But when we live in light of eternity, we can have the courage to persist in any battle that comes our way.

Philippians 3:20-21 says, *"Our citizenship is in heaven. And we eagerly await a Savior from there, the Lord Jesus Christ, who, by the power that enables him to bring everything under his control, will transform our lowly bodies so that they will be like his glorious body"* (NIV).

Take heart, friend. Never give up. Keep swinging for the fence. When you know Jesus Christ, your forever-home is secure.

"Our citizenship is in heaven. And we eagerly await a Savior from there, the Lord Jesus Christ, who, by the power that enables him to bring everything under his control, will transform our lowly bodies so that they will be like his glorious body."

Philippians 3:20-21 NIV

DAY TWENTY-TWO
DON'T BUILD YOUR HOUSE ON SAND

Someday I'd love to build my own house. Whenever I feel like dreaming, I go onto those web sites that show house plans and I imagine myself laying a foundation, putting up the beams and pounding a few nails.

Jesus once told a story about building a house. In His parable He compared a wise man to a foolish man. The wise man represented the person who listened to what Jesus said and followed His advice. The foolish man was the one who heard the same sermon, but decided to ignore the advice.

Jesus said the wise man is like someone who constructed his house on a rock. When the rains came down and the floods came up, the house stood secure. But the foolish is like a man who built his house on sand. When the rains came down and the floods came up, it fell right off its foundation!

Check out the story in Matthew 7. Both men built houses. Both heard the words of Jesus. The wise guy acted according to God's will. But the fool did his own thing.

So, how about you? Are you building your dream house on the sand? Or are you building it on the Rock? Hey, if you've bought the lie from our culture, and you're trying to build your dreams on fame and fortune, let me warn you: *the storm is coming.*

Construct your hopes and dreams on Jesus. Study His Word and listen to what He says. And when the rains come down and the floods come up, your heart will stay strong!

"Therefore everyone who hears these words of mine and puts them into practice is like a wise man who built his house on the rock."

Matthew 7:24 NIV

DAY TWENTY-THREE
JESUS WEPT

Have you ever had a close friend or family member die? It's heartbreaking when someone you love passes away. The amazing thing about Jesus is that He can relate. He knows what it's like to lose a dear friend.

There's a touching story found in John chapter 11. There was city called Bethany located about two miles outside of Jerusalem. Three of Jesus' friends lived in that town: Mary, the one who always sat at Jesus' feet to hear Him teach; her sister Martha, the one who was always busy in the kitchen; and Lazarus, their brother.

Well, Lazarus got really sick—so sick that he actually died. Fast forward, Lazarus had been dead for four days when Jesus finally arrived on the scene. He was moved with compassion for his friends. Most of us have memorized what the Bible said because it's only two words: *"Jesus wept"* (John 11:35 NIV). These two words powerfully express the emotion of His compassion for His friends.

In your grief, remember that Jesus wept. He cried. He cares. He loves you. He understands your sadness.

While you're grieving, remember to keep your hope in the One who loves you enough to weep on your behalf.

Psalm 42:5 says, *"Why are you in despair, O my soul? And why have you become disturbed within me? Hope in God, for I shall again praise Him for the help of His presence"* (NASB).

Make no mistake, my friend. God knows. God is with you. And God cares.

"Why are you in despair, O my soul? And why have you become disturbed within me? Hope in God, for I shall again praise Him for the help of His presence."

Psalm 42:5 NASB

DAY TWENTY-FOUR
FALLING DOWN

We all have moments where we fall down. That's life. Sometimes we fall flat on our faces. But if we fail and give up, we'll never get up!

For me, not having arms and legs makes it a little more difficult to get up. When I was a toddler, I learned how to wriggle my way up from a horizontal position. Even though my parents tried to help me, I had to do it my way. The hard way.

Now and then during a speech, I'll demonstrate the process. It's awkward and anything but graceful. And it's uncomfortable for the audience because they want to rescue me.

Getting up after a fall is a metaphor for life, isn't it? I mean, what feels better? Staying down, or getting up? We weren't meant to stay down! The struggles are meant to help us get stronger and fight for our position. We get resilient when we learn how to overcome the hassles.

Remember Joseph? His brothers betrayed him and sold him into slavery. Later, he was falsely accused by his boss's wife and unfairly tossed into prison and forgotten. But he didn't give up.

Where did Joseph end up? He became the ruler of the highest office in the land. Talk about a comeback!

So, where are you today? Have you fallen down? Begin to see your failures as part of God's gift. He's only making you stronger.

"Then Joseph said to his brothers, 'Come close to me.' When they had done so, he said, 'I am your brother Joseph, the one you sold into Egypt! And now, do not be distressed and do not be angry with yourselves for selling me here, because it was to save lives that God sent me ahead of you. But God sent me ahead of you to preserve for you a remnant on earth and to save your lives by a great deliverance.'"

Genesis 45:4-5, 7 NIV

DAY TWENTY-FIVE
JUST DEAL WITH IT

"Nick, if you want to deal with that pain getting worse and worse for the rest of your life, good luck to you!"

Oh, man. That was not what I wanted to hear. Frankly, I was pretty annoyed to hear George, my physical therapist, give this advice. I met with George to talk about the growing pain in my back. It was getting worse and the issues were multiplying over time. I needed to strengthen my back, but I really wasn't motivated to do the exercises needed.

George's response sounded to me like, *"Nick, you don't have to change if you don't feel like it, but the only person who can help your back feel better is you."*

In Philippians 3, Paul said, *"One thing I do: Forgetting what is behind and straining toward what is ahead, I press on toward the goal to win the prize for which God has called me heavenward in Christ Jesus"* (Philippians 3:13-14 NIV).

Sometimes we resist taking care of our bodies because we're lazy. Or, in my case, I didn't want to exert the energy or press the limits. I didn't really want to sweat.

But sometimes you have to endure a little pain to get healthy.

So, now it's your turn. Are you putting something off? Do you need to address a couple issues in your life that you'd rather ignore? Hey, you won't start to heal until you get to work. Take Paul's advice. Forget the past. Look to the future. And press on toward the goal.

"One thing I do: Forgetting what is behind and straining toward what is ahead, I press on toward the goal to win the prize for which God has called me heavenward in Christ Jesus."

Philippians 3:13-14 NIV

DAY TWENTY-SIX

AN ABUNDANT LIFE

We have so much to be thankful for and so many reasons to be happy. Abundance is everywhere. But look around. Some people actually look depressed!

People often look at my condition and think I've got every reason in the world to be miserable. But I'm not! I have purpose. I have passion. I have joy. I live what Jesus called *an abundant life*. But I'd be lying if I said that my happiness comes from whatever this world offers. In fact, just the opposite is true. Hey, I face tough trials every day, just like you do. But Jesus has given me an awesome gift.

In John 10:10, Jesus said He came *"that [we] may have life, and have it abundantly"* (NASB). Jesus came not only to free us from sin, but to fill all the empty places in our life with meaning. God wants you to experience the thrill of an overflowing life!

My handicap doesn't stop me from doing fun stuff. I surf, I snowboard, I travel, I meet amazing people and I'm always ready for an adventure. God fills my life with grace every single day.

Do you want to know God's purpose for your life? Okay, here it is. God wants you to have a joy-filled abundant life. It doesn't matter who you are or where you're at or what you've done. Jesus came to give you more than you could ever hope for: purpose, love, peace, a life that's full! All you need to do is say, *yes*.

"I came that they may have life, and have it abundantly."

John 10:10 NASB

DAY TWENTY-SEVEN
SHOES IN MY CLOSET

Okay, I got a little confession to make. I may not have arms and legs, but I've got a pair of shoes in my closet!

I'm sure you're familiar with the story by now. My parents had no warning. In fact, three sonograms failed to provide any evidence. So, my condition came as a complete surprise to mum and dad.

From the moment I was born, and even to this day, well-intentioned people prayed for my healing. They ask God to do the impossible and provide a miracle. And believe me, through the years, I've prayed for complete healing, too.

For reasons only God knows, He chose to make me just the way I am. I am perfect in His eyes, and have grown very content with the ridiculously good life He's given me! But even so, I admit, you can still find a pair of shoes in my closet just in case! If God changes His mind, I might need to slip them on and tie the laces!

So, how about you? Have you been hanging on to a dream? Have you been praying for a miracle? Are you hoping for something against all odds? Don't let anyone steal your joy. Let God know the deepest longings of your heart.

Psalm 37:4 says, *"Delight yourself in the LORD; and He will give you the desires of your heart"* (Psalm 37:4 NASB).

Take those symbolic shoes and stick them in the closet. You never know, you might need them someday!

"Delight yourself in the LORD; and He will give you the desires of your heart."

Psalm 37:4 NASB

DAY TWENTY-EIGHT
SMALL IS THE NEW BIG

Bigger is better, so they say. Do you believe that? Bigger cars, bigger houses, even bigger portions at restaurants. As a shorter person, I can tell you that with God, small is the new big.

*Nick, what does **that** mean?*

One day when Jesus was sitting outside the Jewish temple, He saw people give their donations. Jesus watched as rich people came up and dropped large amounts of money into the offering box. Then an old widow came over and slipped in two copper coins. Jesus stood up and turned to His disciples and said, *"This poor widow gave more to the collection than all the others put together"* (Mark 12:43 THE MESSAGE).

Jesus celebrated her small act of generosity. It was more powerful than a million dollar offering because it was accompanied by a lavishly generous heart. You may think your gifts are small, but God doesn't. He calls us to use our gifts to serve others.

Do you like to laugh? Then use your humor to brighten someone's day. Maybe you're a great hugger. Offer comfort to people that are hurting. Or maybe all you can do is paint a fence, sing a song, or sweep a floor. It's time to get busy!

Jesus took a little loaf of bread and some fish and turned them into a feast for thousands. Just watch as He takes your small acts of service and turns them into something great for His glory.

So is bigger better? Not on your life!

"This poor widow gave more to the collection than all the others put together."

Mark 12:43 THE MESSAGE

DAY TWENTY-NINE

YOU MUST BE THIS TALL ...

I was shocked when I finally met John Pingo in person. You would think that appearances wouldn't faze someone like me, right?

Before I had even met John, I heard about the amazing things he was doing in South Africa. Putting his troubled past behind, John became the owner of a small trucking company. But he constantly gave away everything he had to those in need. He was respected and appreciated by everyone in his community. And I was blown away when I finally met him in person.

Why? Well, John Pingo was only nineteen years old! That's right. This awesome missionary was still a teenager. Now that's proof that God doesn't care about age, or our appearance! Everybody and anybody can serve God.

Remember running up to a rollercoaster as a kid, all excited about jumping aboard, only to find the sign that said, *You must be this tall to take the ride?* Here's what God says about rules like that: *"Don't let anyone look down on you because you are young* [or handicapped, or stutter, or any other obstacle], *but set an example for the believers in speech, in conduct, in love, in faith and in purity"* (1 Timothy 4:12 NIV).

Young, old, guy, gal, four limbs, no limbs, it doesn't matter. Don't believe people who say you can't serve God because of this or that. Instead, show them by your actions that God takes all who come. Then, hop on the roller coaster, because serving God is a wild ride!

"Don't let anyone look down on you because you are young, but set an example for the believers in speech, in conduct, in love, in faith and in purity."

---

1 Timothy 4:12 NIV

DAY THIRTY

DARK CLOUDS OF DISCOURAGEMENT

Ever feel down on your luck? Discouraged? Like the dark clouds have moved in over your head, and you can't make them go away?

When I go out in public, it's not unusual to attract some attention. People don't expect to see a grown man without arms or legs. Even more so, they don't expect to see me smiling!

I can hardly say that life is *easy*. Far from it. But I've learned a secret to keeping a positive attitude when those dark clouds move in. It's a powerful weapon called thankfulness.

In 1 Thessalonians 5:18 Paul says, *"In everything give thanks, for this is God's will for you in Christ Jesus"* (NASB). When we start to dwell on the things we don't have, we can get miserable really quick. But when we think about all the things we do have, it can change our perspective entirely!

First of all, if you're a follower of Jesus Christ, we can be thankful for a God who knows our deepest secrets and still loves us. Second, we can be thankful for life.

Every breath we take is a gift. And finally, we can be thankful for others—our friends, family and brothers and sisters in Christ.

If you've fallen into a blue funk and you can't seem to pull yourself out, make a deliberate effort to focus and reflect on God's many gifts to you. Start saying *thank you*. As you do, it won't be long before those dark ominous clouds are replaced by sunny blue skies.

"In everything give thanks, for this is God's will for you in Christ Jesus."

1 Thessalonians 5:18 NASB

DAY THIRTY-ONE
GETTING THE BIG PICTURE

So, how's your day going? Is there a lot on your to-do list?

It's easy to get caught up in the craziness of the day, to look at the urgent things right in front of us instead of stepping back to see the big picture. I do it all the time. I need a caregiver to help me do daily things like brush my teeth or lift me into a wheelchair, and if I dwell on the daily tasks that have to get done and all the stuff I can't do by myself, I run the risk of going into a downward spiral.

In the great book of poetry right in the middle of the Bible called Psalms, there's a reminder that goes like this: *"Lord, You have been our dwelling place in all generations. Before the mountains were born, or You gave birth to the earth and the world, even from everlasting to everlasting, You are God"* (Psalm 90:1-2 NASB).

When I ponder those verses, everything I worry about gets snuffed out! My worries today or this week, this month or even this year pale in comparison to that powerful line: *"God is God, from everlasting to everlasting."*

Maybe that's what you need to remember today. God is bigger than our silly to-do list. Bigger than the annoying neighbor three doors down. Bigger than the upcoming job interview. Bigger than the financial crunch facing you this month. With the Psalmist, we can say, *"From everlasting to everlasting, You are God."*

So, how's your day going?

"Lord, You have been our dwelling place in all generations. Before the mountains were born, or You gave birth to the earth and the world, even from everlasting to everlasting, You are God."

Psalm 90:1-2 NASB